DYNAMIC DUOS OF SCIENCE

JANE GOODALL
AND
MARY LEAKEY

W
FRANKLIN WATTS
LONDON · SYDNEY

Matt Anniss

Franklin Watts
First published in Great Britain in 2016 by The Watts Publishing Group

Credits
Produced by Calcium
Series Editors: Sarah Eason and Jennifer Sanderson
Series Designer: Keith Williams
Picture researcher: Rachel Blount

Photo credits: Cover: The Leakey Foundation (right), Wikimedia Commons: Jeekc (left), Guérin Nicolas (background); Inside: Corbis: Bettmann 15; Dreamstime: 3drenderings 18, Nebojsa Babic 29b, Daniel Bellhouse 30, Rafał Cichawa 23, Eduardo Gonzalez Diaz 29t, Eric Gevaert 1, 16, Udomsak Insome 26, Isselee 36, Ivkuzmin 32, Kmiragaya 27, Chris Kruger 14, Xavier Marchant 28, Mattiaath 25, Pat Olson 31, Leung Cho Pan 22, Prillfoto 12, Peter Spirer 9, Waxart 37; Flickr: Kristoffer Tripplaar/World Bank 21; Sarah Peutrill 10; Shutterstock: Aaron Amat 33, Nick Biemans 45, Zbynek Burival 34, Kjersti Joergensen 4, Kletr 17, Lmfoto 7, Moizhusein 19b, Natursports 8, Robin Nieuwenkamp 6, Ferenc Szelepcsenyi 5b, Kirsanov Valeriy Vladimirovich 35; The Leakey Foundation: 5t; Wikimedia Commons: Csigabi 44, Tim Evanson 38, Ikiwaner 19t, 20, Jeekc 43, Michaelagray 24, Momotarou2012 39, Guérin Nicolas 3, Nrkpan 13, 40, Ed Schipul 41, Smithsonian Institution Archives 11, William Waterway 42.

Dewey number: 576.8'0922
ISBN: 978 1 4451 4481 8

Printed in China

MIX
Paper from
responsible sources
FSC® C104740
FSC www.fsc.org

Franklin Watts
An imprint of
Hachette Children's Group
Part of The Watts Publishing Group
Carmelite House
50 Victoria Embankment
London EC4Y 0DZ

An Hachette UK Company
www.hachette.co.uk

www.franklinwatts.co.uk

Contents

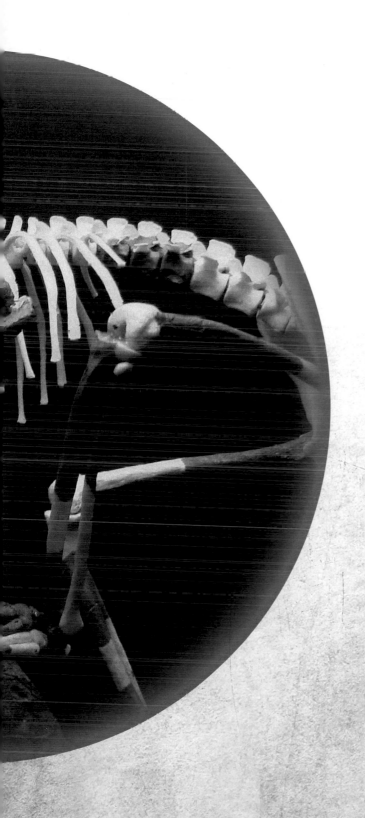

CHAPTER 1

An Alliance of Understanding

In 1859, the British scientist Charles Darwin published a book called *On the Origin of Species*. In it Darwin proposed that humans and apes shared a common ancestor. He put forwards the theory of evolution, which stated that over millions of years life-forms adapt and change to suit their environment.

When Darwin's work was published, his ideas were criticised because they suggested an alternative to the Christian belief that God created the world. People demanded proof that they were related to monkeys, and asked what aspects of ape behaviour suggested a close link with humans.

Darwin's research into apes such as chimpanzees paved the way for later scientists to further investigate human origins.

Increasing understanding

In the twentieth century, a group of scientists began searching for answers to the questions posed by the publication of *On the Origin of Species*. Among the scientists were Mary Nicol, who later became known as Mary Leakey, and Jane Goodall. Mary was an archaeologist who specialised in searching for remains of early humans. Jane Goodall is a researcher who has devoted her life to studying the behaviour of chimpanzees, the ape thought to be man's closest living relative. Over the course of 50 years, Mary and Jane's discoveries have revolutionised the way that people think about evolution, increased scientists' understanding of man's earliest ancestors and proved that humans and apes are not so different after all.

Although Mary Leakey (top) and Jane Goodall (bottom) did not work together directly, they will always be strongly linked thanks to the connected nature of their scientific research.

BEHIND THE SCIENCE

Archaeology is the study of human activity from the distant past. Archaeologists search for objects buried in the ground that are hundreds, thousands or even millions of years old. By examining them, they can then explain what the remains tell people about their ancestors.

Mary's Early Life

Jane Goodall and Mary Nicol had vastly different childhoods. Goodall was also born much later than Nicol, at a time when Nicol was just beginning her career as an archaeologist.

Mary Douglas Nicol was born on the 6th February, 1913, in London. She was the daughter of the painter Erskine Nicol and his wife Cecilia. The nature of Erskine's work meant that the family moved around, living in countries including the United States, Italy and Egypt. The Nicol family spent most of its summers in the south of France where Erskine would paint pictures of their surroundings.

The rich prehistoric history of Les Eyzies in the Dordogne region of France, where Mary spent the summer of 1925, had an enormous impact on her life and her future choice of career.

It was finding exciting objects such as this prehistoric axe head, crafted by hand from flint by one of our ancestors, that first ignited Mary's interest in archaeology. At the end of every summer holiday, she returned home to England with boxes full of treasures such as this.

Searching for evidence

In the summer of 1925, when Mary was 12, her family stayed in Les Eyzies, a town in the Dordogne, in France, famous for its ancient caves. At the time, the French archaeologist Elie Peyrony (1897–1989) was looking for objects in these caves, which hundreds of thousands of years ago had been home to early humans. Mary was fascinated by Peyrony's work, and asked for permission to search through the pile of objects the archaeologist had found and discarded. She found many interesting artefacts, enough to begin her own collection of prehistoric objects. Mary's lifelong love of archaeology had begun.

BEHIND THE SCIENCE

When scientists and historians talk about the 'prehistoric' period, they are referring to any time before humans began to write records. The first written documents date from about 5,400 years ago.

School Days

Mary did not like school very much and regularly argued with her teachers. Every day, she could not wait for school to finish so she could return home and pursue her interests in drawing and archaeology.

While in France on her summer holidays, Mary had the opportunity to watch an archaeological dig, like the one shown below. She found it fascinating, and vowed to devote her life to digging for traces of our ancestors.

When Mary was 13 years old, her father died of cancer. The family moved back to London and Mary was sent to a local Catholic school. She did not enjoy her new school. Despite speaking French well, her teachers criticised the way she spoke it. Mary found her English class just as challenging, and was finally expelled from the school after refusing to recite a poem.

Mary was never officially a student at University College London and never took any exams, but the college's rules allowed her to sit in on classes to learn more about archaeology.

Bad grades

Mary was then sent to a second Catholic school but things did not turn out well there either. One day during a science lesson, she managed to cause a small explosion while carrying out a chemistry experiment. Her teachers were not impressed and she was expelled for a second time.

Cecilia Nicol decided to employ tutors to teach her daughter, but Mary still showed little sign of improvement. Her mother had hoped that Mary would go to the University of Oxford but she was denied a place because her grades were not good enough. Instead, Mary began to attend archaeology classes at University College London and the London Museum. Mary quickly realised that to achieve her dream of a career as an archaeologist, she would have to find work on an archaeological dig and prove that she had what it took to succeed.

IN THEIR OWN WORDS

Mary hated school. She said:

'I had never passed a single school exam, and clearly never would.'

A Talent for Drawing

In 1932, Mary found work on an archaeological dig for the first time. She left London for St Albans, north of London, to search for Roman treasures under the leadership of one of her teachers at the London Museum, Mortimer Wheeler (1890–1976).

After this period, Mary found work on another dig in Hembury, in the south-west of England. There she helped unearth many prehistoric items. She was a talented artist and regularly made sketches of her finds. The lead archaeologist on the dig, Dorothy Liddell, noticed Mary's illustrations and asked her to draw the prehistoric tools found on the dig.

Mary could not have asked for a greater place than St Albans for her first archaeological dig. In Roman times, it was the site of Verulamium, the second-largest Roman town in Britain.

A shared love of natural history brought Mary and Louis together. This shared passion helped them to become one of the most successful partnerships in the history of archaeology.

Meeting Louis

Mary's sketches also caught the eye of another archaeologist, Gertrude Caton-Thompson (1888–1985). This led to an introduction to Louis Leakey (1903–1972). It was not long before he asked the young archaeologist to provide drawings for a book about early humans, based on his archaeological finds. The book was called *Adam's Ancestors*, and through working on it together, Louis and Mary fell in love. Louis and Mary were both free spirits with a sense of adventure and a dislike of rules. They were passionate about the story of human evolution and the plight of animals. In 1936, Louis and Mary married.

IN THEIR OWN WORDS

About her work, Mary said:

'I dug things up. I was curious. I liked to draw what I found.'

The 16-Million-Year-Old Ape

The Leakeys' first adventure as a married couple was to move to Olduvai Gorge in Tanzania, in eastern Africa. They wanted to find evidence of man's earliest ancestors and Africa seemed the right place to begin their search.

Almost immediately, they began to uncover evidence of early human settlements, discovering basic chopping tools made of stone. They also conducted digs in Kenya and it was at Olorgesailie, near Nairobi, that Mary made her first big discovery – the remains of an early human settlement. Some of the astonishing objects the Leakeys discovered there were between 1.2 million and 400,000 years old.

The barren, dry land around Olorgesailie in Kenya has proved to be a treasure trove for archaeologists over the years. It is particularly famous for the number of prehistoric hand tools, especially axes, which have been found there.

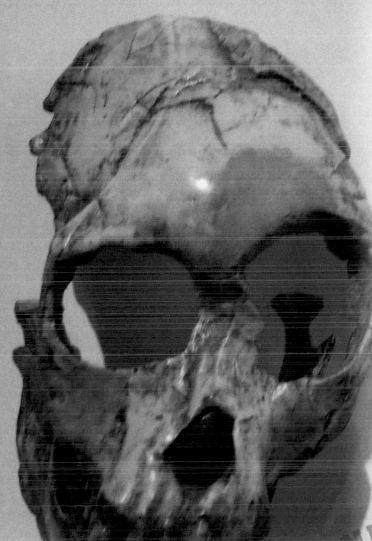

Historic finds

In 1948, the Leakeys made their second staggering discovery. While searching on Rusinga Island in Lake Victoria, Kenya, they began to find what appeared to be tiny fragments of an ancient skull. The Leakeys had discovered what became known as *Proconsul africanus*, the skull of a creature that lived between 15 and 25 million years ago and was a direct ancestor of modern apes and humans. It was the first near-complete ape skull ever to be found, and the Leakeys' discovery made the news across the world.

The Proconsul africanus skull discovered by the Leakeys was significant because it proved that humans and modern apes shared common ancestors, with distinctive features found in both species.

BEHIND THE SCIENCE

The Leakeys were able to discover the skull because its bones had been naturally preserved through fossilisation. In the fossilisation process, the remains of an animal or human survive, usually underground, for hundreds of thousands or millions of years.

CHAPTER 2

New Discoveries

Following their great discovery on Rusinga Island the Leakeys met a wildlife enthusiast named Jane Goodall. Jane Goodall was born in London in 1934. At the same time that the Leakeys began to work together, Goodall was taking her very first steps as a toddler!

Before Goodall could walk, her father gave her a toy monkey, which he named Jubilee. To this day, the stuffed toy remains one of Goodall's most treasured possessions and sits on the dressing table in her bedroom.

From an early age Goodall was fascinated by wildlife of all shapes and sizes, from African elephants and giraffes, to the birds that would fly into the back garden of her family home in London.

The inspirational toy

Playing with Jubilee sparked Goodall's interest in animals. As she grew up, she began to take more interest in nature, and would spend her spare time observing birds and animals. Goodall made a point of reading everything she could about wildlife, and dreamt of one day travelling to Africa to observe exotic animals, particularly monkeys, up close. After she left school in 1952, Goodall worked two jobs to fund her dream. During the day she was a secretary in Oxford, while at night and on weekends she worked for a documentary film company in London.

By 1957, Goodall had saved enough money to travel to Kenya, where she stayed on a friend's farm. It would prove to be a trip that changed Goodall's life forever.

As a young woman, Goodall was determined to work with animals and had a particular fascination with apes.

IN THEIR OWN WORDS

Goodall said:

'My mother's friends were horrified by my toy monkey, thinking it would frighten me and give me nightmares.'

A Fateful Phone Call

When she arrived in Kenya, Goodall read a newspaper article about an archaeologist called Louis Leakey, who had taken a part-time job as curator of the Coryndon Museum in Nairobi.

Louis had become known for his interest in early humans, animals and evolution, so Goodall decided to contact Leakey to ask for an appointment with him to discuss his work. Louis was surprised by the call, but it gave him an idea.

Louis knew that archaeology alone could not answer the big questions about human evolution, and wondered whether studying the behaviour of our nearest relatives, chimpanzees, might help.

The great test

For a long time, Louis had believed that close study of ape behaviour could help scientists understand more about human evolution. More importantly, it could also give him clues about how early humans, who were more closely related to apes than modern humans, behaved. This type of research would tie in perfectly with the Leakeys' tireless quest to study prehistoric humans. After talking the idea through, the Leakeys offered Goodall a job as a secretary. It was a test to see if Goodall had the temperament, drive and the ambition to study chimpanzees in the wild. Goodall passed the test with flying colours.

BEHIND THE SCIENCE

The creatures most closely related to humans are chimpanzees. We now know that the deoxyribonucleic acid (DNA) of *Homo sapiens* (the scientific name for humans) and *Pan troglodytes* (chimpanzees) is up to 98.4 percent identical. Humans and chimpanzees must share the same common ancestors.

Meet the Ancestors

In 1959, at Olduvai Gorge, Mary made one of the greatest archaeological finds of the twentieth century. It was another fossilised skull, but this time it was even more remarkable than the remains of the ape she had found 11 years earlier.

The remains of the skull were found in the form of many more fragments, scattered over an area a metre or so wide. After painstakingly putting the pieces back together, Mary named the skull *Zinjanthropus*. Further research proved that the skull was around 1.7 million years old. Amazingly, Mary had not found an ancestor of both apes and humans, but an early human. Further investigation revealed that the skull came from a species of human that died out around 1.5 million years ago.

This is a computer-generated recreation of the skull and skeleton of Zinjanthropus. *Although significantly different from a twenty-first century human, with a more pronounced jaw and smaller, flatter skull, the 1.5 million-year-old skeleton looks far more like a human than an ape.*

Spreading the news

News of Mary's discovery spread around the world. As a result of the couple's newly found fame, Louis raised more money to fund their research. The extra funding also helped to pay for Louis' other project: Goodall's study of chimpanzee behaviour. In 1958, Louis had sent Goodall to London to learn more about apes under the tuition of Osman Hill (1901–1975) and John Napier (1917–1987) at London Zoo and Kings College. In 1960, Louis asked Goodall to travel to Gombe Stream National Park in Tanzania to begin her study of chimpanzees in the wild.

The way chimps behave is similar to early humans. Their simple, human-like forms of behaviour, as first seen by Goodall, provide a link to the past and show what our prehistoric ancestors may have been like.

BEHIND THE SCIENCE

Millions of years ago, various species of human beings, called hominids, existed, all with different bodies and physical capabilities. *Australopithecus zinjanthropus* was one of these species. Others included *Homo erectus* and *Homo habilis*, fossilised bones of which were discovered for the first time by Mary and Louis in 1960.

CHAPTER 3

Living With Chimps

In 1960, Goodall arrived at Gombe Stream National Park in Tanzania ready to begin her study of chimpanzees. It was the beginning of what would become a lifelong study. In 2000, she published a book marking 40 years of work at the nature reserve.

Back in 1960, Goodall had no idea how long she would be based at Gombe Stream. She knew that it could take a long time to make the observations necessary to gather new information about the way chimpanzees behaved.

Goodall's accommodation at Gombe Stream was cramped and very basic, with few modern amenities. However, she did not mind because it allowed her to be close to nature, and the chimpanzees she loved so dearly.

Goodall is now respected the world over for the unique bond she developed with the chimps at Gombe Stream. Here Goodall is giving a talk on her work at the World Bank's Preston Auditorium, hosted by Inger Andersen (right).

A difficult task

From the beginning, Goodall's work was challenging All previous attempts by scientists to study chimpanzees in the wild had failed. The apes either behaved unnaturally when researchers appeared, fled or were frightened away by the off-road cars the researchers used to follow the creatures.

Louis was convinced that Goodall had what it took to successfully study chimpanzee behaviour, a view shared by Mary. He knew she was patient, loved the outdoors and did not mind spending long periods of time alone. The chimpanzee study was vitally important to Louis and Mary. They both wanted to understand more about how human ancestors, who slowly evolved from great apes over millions of years, lived their lives. By studying chimpanzees closely, Louis and Mary believed that Goodall could answer many of the questions posed by those who doubted the theory of evolution.

IN THEIR OWN WORDS

Goodall said:

'Given that chimpanzees and many other animals are sentient and sapient, we should treat them with respect.'

Watching and Waiting

Goodall's life at Gombe Stream was simple. She lived in a camp by the shores of Lake Tanganyika, and every morning would travel into a little patch of forest where Gombe Stream's small community of chimpanzees lived. Goodall would then sit and watch the chimpanzees for up to 12 hours, making detailed notes about what they did, how they behaved and their daily routine.

Goodall found it very difficult to observe the chimpanzees at close quarters. Every time she tried to get within 500 metres of the animals, they would run away. For a researcher whose life revolved around studying chimpanzees, it was a demoralising experience.

Scientists now believe that early humans stopped walking on all fours like this chimpanzee when they realised that walking upright would save energy that could be used for hunting and other tiring tasks.

Goodall's base was in a beautiful location by the shores of Lake Tanganyika in Tanzania. Like Mary Leakey, Goodall lived a simple life during her time in Africa.

A slow process

In 1961, a year after setting foot in Gombe Stream, Goodall decided to find another chimpanzee group to follow, which eventually accepted her presence. At the same time every morning, she would appear in the same place, close to the Kakombe Stream valley. Within one year, the chimpanzees allowed her to come within 30 metres of the group. With each passing month, the chimpanzees grew more accustomed to Goodall. Eventually, they welcomed her into their group, and she became the first human to be accepted by apes in this way.

BEHIND THE SCIENCE

Unlike many other apes and monkeys, chimpanzees can stand and walk on two legs, just like humans. However, most of the time, they walk on all fours, using both their arms and legs. This technique is called 'knuckle walking'.

23

Unusual Methods

Goodall approached her research differently to other scientists. Most scientists prefer to keep some distance from their subjects. In previous studies of chimpanzees, the scientists had given the apes code numbers. The scientists watched from a distance and did not attempt to bond with the animals in any way.

Goodall believed studying chimpanzees remotely was too impersonal and she gave the animals she observed names. By doing so, she found it easier to recognise the chimpanzee's individual character traits.

For example, she named the first male chimpanzee that warmed to her 'David Greybeard', and one of the stronger males was named 'Goliath'.

The fame of David Greybeard, the first chimp to respond to Goodall at Gombe Stream, has spread worldwide thanks to this wood carving on the Tree of Life in the Animal Kingdom theme park at Walt Disney World in Florida.

Goodall noticed that chimps show many signs of human behaviour, such as living in families and youngsters playing together, just like children.

An emotional attachment

Over time, Goodall was able to forge strong bonds with the chimpanzees she studied. This led to criticism of Goodall by some scientists, who said that her observations were clouded by her emotional attachment to the Gombe Stream chimpanzees. Despite the criticisms, Goodall proved that her methods worked. She managed to get closer to chimpanzees than any human had before or since, giving her a unique insight into how the animals behave. Her methods resulted in observations that have forever changed our understanding of the way chimpanzees – and, by extension, early humans – live their lives.

IN THEIR OWN WORDS

When she began her work at Gombe Stream, Goodall had no scientific training. Leakey helped her gain a place at Cambridge University. She said:

'I wanted to get a university degree because Louis Leakey said I needed one, and once I succeeded I could get back to Gombe Stream.'

CHAPTER 4
Chimpanzees and Humans

Like the Leakeys, Goodall was interested in learning about the similarities between chimpanzees and humans. For example, could the animals communicate with each other, as humans do when talking? Were they intelligent enough to use basic tools? Like humans, did they live as families and use close contact to show affection towards each other?

Chimpanzee troops are loosely based around family groups. Just like human families, each member has a role in the group, from the older females who act as wise mentors to the adult males who behave as dominant leaders.

It took Goodall a long time to find answers to her questions and she went to extraordinary lengths to gain the trust of the chimpanzee group. Goodall climbed into trees to spend time with the chimpanzees, ate the same foods as them and mimicked some of their behaviour.

Chimpanzees have a basic language that is similar to that which our human ancestors may have used.

Answers to questions

Over the 40-year period Goodall spent living with the chimpanzees at Gombe Stream, she got extremely close to her subjects. As a result, she witnessed first-hand chimpanzee behaviour that other scientists had never seen, including traits and characteristics that were similar to those seen in humans. One of her most startling discoveries was about the way chimpanzees communicate. Previously, scientists had thought that there was no logic to the sounds the apes made when they were spending time with each other. After years of watching and listening, Goodall concluded that chimpanzees use 20 different sounds to communicate.

BEHIND THE SCIENCE

Chimpanzees live in groups called troops. A chimpanzee troop can have between 15 and 120 members, very much like an extended human family. Each troop has a mix of males, females and offspring of different ages.

Chimps Are Individuals

Goodall's relationship with the chimpanzees allowed her a unique and amazingly intimate access to the animals. Through this, she came to a startling conclusion: like humans, chimpanzees have very distinct personalities.

Each person has characteristics that are different from those of another person. Some people are bubbly and enthusiastic; others are shy and quiet, and just want to fit in with the group. Chimpanzees are no different to humans in this respect.

Goodall discovered that the chimps at Gombe Stream had very distinct personalities, which varied enormously. Some were quiet and introspective, while others were lively. Some were even loud and angry.

Human behaviour

Over years, Goodall began to notice the differences seen in human characteristics in the chimpanzees. The chimpanzee she named Goliath was loud and bold, and spent a period of time as the troop's unofficial leader. Another chimpanzee, 'Auntie Flo', was incapable of having any offspring, but was often seen putting an arm around younger members of the troop, as if to give them support. Over time, Goodall noticed the chimpanzees showing 'human behaviour', such as hugs, kisses and pats on the back. She also saw chimpanzees playfully tickling each other.

Goodall also saw the chimpanzees displaying emotions, something scientists previously thought only humans were capable of. Mary Leakey was particularly excited by Goodall's discoveries because they suggested a much closer link between chimps and humans – and, by extension, their distant ancestors – than scientists had previously thought.

IN THEIR OWN WORDS

On the apes' behaviour, Goodall said:

'It is not only human beings who have personality, who are capable of rational thought and emotions like joy and sorrow.'

Just as you can tell the way one of your friends is feeling by looking at his or her face, you can 'read' a chimp's emotions simply by looking at its facial expressions.

Not Just Vegetarians

One day in 1960, while she watched the chimpanzees at Gombe Stream, Goodall noticed something extraordinary. One of the chimpanzees was dipping a grass stalk into a termite mound to attract the tiny insects. The termites clung on to the grass, making it easier for the chimpanzee to eat them.

Although it seems a small action, it was a significant discovery – the chimpanzee was hunting the termites, using the grass as an improvised fishing rod to hook out the insects. Goodall had witnessed one of the first signs of chimpanzees using tools, a significantly human-like action. Excited by her discovery, Goodall began to watch the chimpanzees for signs of similar behaviour. On several occasions, she noticed them snapping off twigs and stripping the leaves from trees to make better tools for catching termites. These examples of chimpanzee intelligence and improvisation were revolutionary discoveries that helped further link the ancestry of modern humans to chimpanzees.

Just as humans have evolved over thousands of years, scientists believe that chimps are also slowly evolving. This means that in hundreds of thousands of years, chimpanzees may be capable of more complex, human-like tasks.

Hunter-gatherers

At the time of Goodall's studies, most scientists believed that chimpanzees were not intelligent enough to make and use basic tools. In fact, they thought that using tools was the main action that made humans different from apes. Scientists also believed that, unlike humans, chimpanzees did not have an instinct to hunt. However, Goodall had seen that by fishing for termites, chimpanzees were undertaking a very basic form of hunting. Finally, the fact that the chimpanzees ate insects disproved the former scientific belief that chimpanzees were vegetarians.

When Louis and Mary learned of Goodall's findings, they were delighted. Goodall had proved that chimpanzees were hunters that used tools to catch and eat other living creatures, just like man's earliest ancestors.

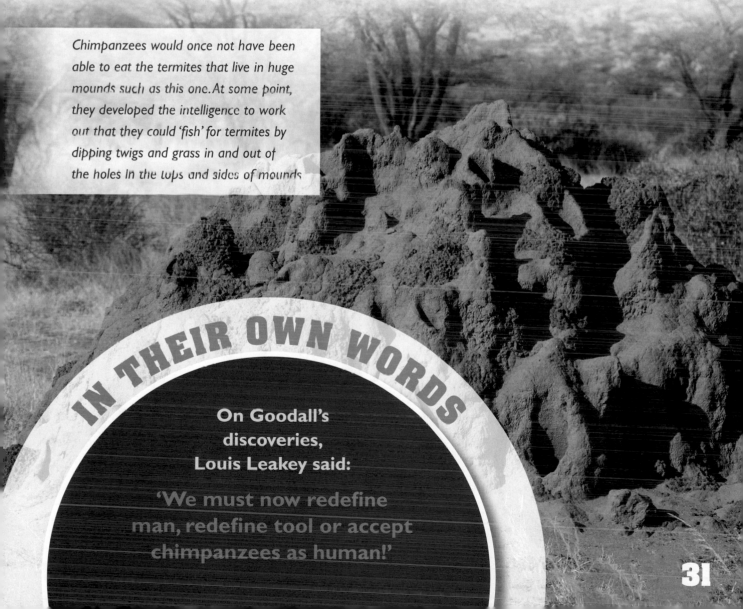

Chimpanzees would once not have been able to eat the termites that live in huge mounds such as this one. At some point, they developed the intelligence to work out that they could 'fish' for termites by dipping twigs and grass in and out of the holes in the tops and sides of mounds.

IN THEIR OWN WORDS

On Goodall's discoveries, Louis Leakey said:

'We must now redefine man, redefine tool or accept chimpanzees as human!'

31

Chimps Can Be Aggressive

Before Goodall began her study at Gombe Stream, scientists, including Goodall, believed that chimpanzees were peace-loving animals that did not show any signs of aggression. Like other researchers, Goodall believed that our human ancestors' love of hunting and fighting were features that developed following their evolution from apes millions of years ago. As it turned out, she was wrong.

Goodall witnessed chimpanzees fighting each other and one chimpanzee, the most dominant male in the group, attacked her on a number of occasions. In another breakthrough, Goodall witnessed male chimpanzees hunting, killing and eating colobus monkeys. They trapped the monkeys in the trees so that they could not get away, before killing them. The meat of the dead monkey was then shared around the troop.

The chimps at Gombe Stream work in groups, just like early human hunter-gatherers, to kill up to one-third of the park's population of colobus monkeys every year.

Goodall was the first scientist to observe that chimpanzees are occasionally aggressive, just like humans. Goodall was initially both shocked and surprised by the discovery.

Hunters and killers

On another occasion, Goodall saw some of the chimpanzees kill and eat another chimpanzee. Finding out that the chimps were not the peace-loving animals she believed them to be was very difficult for Goodall to accept. What she saw, however, did offer more proof of the links between chimpanzees and early humans. Millions of years ago, man's ancestors hunted in groups, just as chimpanzees hunt.

IN THEIR OWN WORDS

On the chimps' aggressive behaviour, Goodall said:

'It was both fascinating and appalling to learn that chimpanzees were capable of hostile behaviour that was not unlike certain forms of primitive human warfare.'

Man's Closest Relatives

Goodall's discoveries changed scientists' understanding of chimpanzees, and gave them more clues about how man's distant ancestors may have behaved. Her discovery that chimpanzees were capable of creating very basic tools from grass and twigs offered a link to a common ancestor from which both humans and chimps evolved. Scientists now believe that chimps and humans began to diverge from a common ancestor more than 10 million years ago.

While Goodall was researching the chimpanzees at Gombe Stream, elsewhere in Tanzania, Mary Leakey was continuing her own quest for further knowledge of man's ancestry. Like Goodall, Mary, too was continuing to find evidence that strengthened the links between man's ancestors and other great apes. In 1960, when she discovered the skull of *Homo habilis* alongside Louis, she also found remains of simple stone tools.

The discovery of the Homo habilis skull buried with basic stone tools proved that in the years between early humans and chimpanzees developing into different species, humans had developed the ability to manufacture tools.

Today, archaeologists continue to carry out the slow, methodical process of excavating a site, with the hope of finding more buried clues about our distant prehistoric ancestors.

Just like man

This was a leap forwards in the evolutionary story. Earlier in 1960, Goodall had spotted one of her chimps, David Greybeard, using twigs and grass to 'fish' for termites. The early human discovered by the Leakeys had moved on from simple 'termite fishing' to actually hunting and killing other animals using simple stone tools of his own creation. The ape-like *Homo habilis* showed more human characteristics than any of man's earlier, ape-like ancestors. It was another important stage in the evolution of the human race. In the years to come, Mary would uncover even more dramatic evidence of man's ape-like ancestors, increasing scientists' understanding of the story of human development.

BEHIND THE SCIENCE

In 2007, scientists from Iowa State University and the University of Cambridge watched chimpanzees create spears from tree branches. The apes used their teeth to sharpen one end of each branch to make it more like the spears man's ancestors used when hunting prey.

Walking in Their Footsteps

Like Goodall, Mary was happiest when she was working in Tanzania. Mary once said that she was happier living in a tent than in a house. She loved to live 'out in the field', close to the many archaeological sites at Olduvai Gorge.

In 1972, Louis passed away. In the last few years of his life, he and Mary had been separated. The couple had been growing apart for many years. Louis travelled the world raising money and giving talks on their findings while Mary stayed in Olduvai Gorge to hunt for more remains.

Eventually, Mary had grown tired of Louis's 'celebrity lifestyle' and constant desire to turn their work into front-page news. Mary was still fascinated by her archaeological digs and realised that there was still much for her to discover about human ancestry.

Mary lived a very simple life in Africa, and regularly talked about how she loved sleeping in a tent, under the stars.

Fossils such as this ammonite can tell scientists about the history of Earth, its earliest inhabitants and even humankind itself.

BEHIND THE SCIENCE

It is possible for scientists to work out exactly how old fossils are using a process called potassium-argon dating. By comparing the amount of argon and potassium in a fossil, it is possible to accurately date objects that are millions of years old.

A family business

By the 1970s, archaeology had become a Leakey family pursuit. Mary and Louis' sons Richard (born 1944) and Jonathan (born 1940) worked alongside her at Olduvai Gorge. They were present one day in 1978, when one of Mary's team excitedly called her over to a patch of ground the team had been excavating on the Laetoli Plains. There, hidden under a layer of ash, was what looked like the fossilised remains of a series of footprints.

Landmark Discovery

Mary was incredibly excited by the finding of the footprints in Tanzania. As she knelt down to inspect the prints that had been hidden in the mud for millions of years, her face lit up with a smile. Realising the importance of the discovery, she stood up and said: 'Now this is really something to put on the mantelpiece!'

Mary knew that the footprints belonged to some of man's earliest ancestors. Over the next few weeks her team uncovered a trail of footprints that stretched for more than 26 metres. There were three sets of footprints, suggesting they belonged to a male, female and child. Scientists later worked out that the footprints were 3.6 million years old. This made them the oldest footprints ever discovered.

This is a stone cast of the footprints found by Mary Leakey's team in the ground at Laetoli. To this day, they remain the earliest known human footprints ever discovered.

Upright man

Mary could tell from the footprints that these ape-like ancestors were walking upright, just like humans, rather than knuckle walking like chimpanzees and gorillas. Scientists had previously thought that early humans began walking on two feet much more recently than 3.6 million years ago. Proof that man's chimpanzee-like ancestors could walk on two feet revolutionised people's ideas about man's evolution.

The Laetoli footprints remain one of the most sensational archaeological finds of all time. They are so significant, that they have been protected for future generations by the Tanzanian government.

The original Laetoli footprints are now protected for future generations by a strong, thick layer of protective glass. They may be 3.6 million years old, but without proper protection they could be worn away by the elements.

IN THEIR OWN WORDS

About the footprints, Mary said:

'I think the footprints are the most important find in view of human evolution. I was really looking for tools, but I never found any at the site.'

CHAPTER 6

Lasting Legacies

Following their landmark discoveries, Mary Leakey and Jane Goodall continued to work in their fields. Such was their devotion to their respective professions, they both continued working into old age.

Following her great discovery at Laetoli, Mary Leakey wrote a book about her life as an archaeologist in Africa, entitled *Olduvai Gorge: My Search for Early Man.* Alongside her team, she continued to work on uncovering the footprint trail at Laetoli until 1981.

In 1985, Mary's son, Richard, discovered the almost complete skull of a previously unknown human ancestor in Kenya. It was named Australopithecus aethiopicus *and was some 2.5 million years old.*

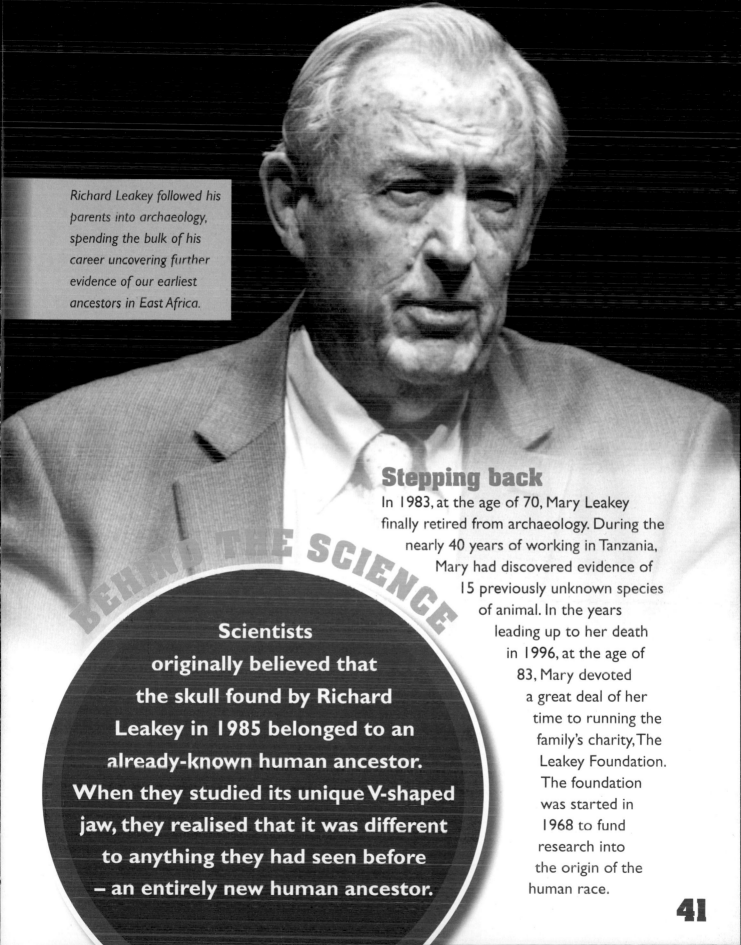

Richard Leakey followed his parents into archaeology, spending the bulk of his career uncovering further evidence of our earliest ancestors in East Africa.

BEHIND THE SCIENCE

Stepping back

In 1983, at the age of 70, Mary Leakey finally retired from archaeology. During the nearly 40 years of working in Tanzania, Mary had discovered evidence of 15 previously unknown species of animal. In the years leading up to her death in 1996, at the age of 83, Mary devoted a great deal of her time to running the family's charity, The Leakey Foundation. The foundation was started in 1968 to fund research into the origin of the human race.

Scientists originally believed that the skull found by Richard Leakey in 1985 belonged to an already-known human ancestor. When they studied its unique V-shaped jaw, they realised that it was different to anything they had seen before – an entirely new human ancestor.

Championing Chimpanzees

Since the 1970s, Goodall has refocused her attention from studying the chimpanzees at Gombe Stream to fighting to protect chimpanzees and their habitats. Although chimpanzees are a protected species, illegal hunters continue to target them. In some African countries, chimpanzee meat and fur can change hands for large sums of money.

To help protect wildlife and support research into chimpanzee behaviour, Goodall founded the Jane Goodall Institute in 1977. The organisation now has 28 offices around the world, holds an archive of Goodall's notes and photographs from her years of research at Gombe Stream (currently based at Duke University, North Carolina) and a youth wing.

Goodall now spends much of her time working with young people, helping them learn more about chimpanzees and other wildlife. Here, she is seen talking to children in the United States.

A charity for young people

Roots and Shoots, the institute's conservation charity for young people, was founded in 1991, after 12 teenagers visited Goodall's home to ask what they could do to help protect chimpanzees. More than 20 years later, there are over 150,000 Roots and Shoots members in more than 130 countries around the world.

Goodall now spends most of her time travelling the world, talking to people about the plight of her beloved chimpanzees. In 2004, the Queen honoured Goodall for her years of research and campaigning, by naming her Dame Jane Goodall.

IN THEIR OWN WORDS

Goodall said:

'Chimpanzees have been living for hundreds of thousands of years in their forest, living fantastic lives, never overpopulating, never destroying the forest. I would say they have been way more successful than us.'

Dynamic Differences

Mary Leakey and Jane Goodall were remarkable scientists. Although they never worked together, they will forever be linked through Mary's husband, Louis. He introduced the two women in 1958, and raised hundreds of thousands of pounds to help fund both scientists' work.

Although very different, Mary and Jane shared many character traits. Both came from outside the world of science, with no university qualifications, to achieve great things and become respected scientists. Both were dedicated to their work, living for many years in isolation in Africa. Both understood that learning more about chimpanzee behaviour would help piece together the story of human evolution.

Goodall's lasting legacy is not only her groundbreaking research, but also the way she has inspired an entire new generation of young people to take an interest in protecting chimpanzees and their habitats.

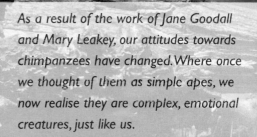

As a result of the work of Jane Goodall and Mary Leakey, our attitudes towards chimpanzees have changed. Where once we thought of them as simple apes, we now realise they are complex, emotional creatures, just like us.

Solving the evolution puzzle

Few people have done more to put together the pieces of the evolutionary puzzle than Mary Leakey and Jane Goodall. Mary uncovered evidence of man's earliest ancestors, charting the development of man from simple apes to complex human beings. Goodall's long study of chimpanzee behaviour proved that we are more similar to great apes than scientists once thought, giving vital clues about how human ancestors may have behaved. Thanks to the work of Goodall and Leakey, the human evolution puzzle is now a far more complete picture.

IN THEIR OWN WORDS

Mary said:

'There is still so much underground at Olduvai Gorge. It is a vast place, and there is plenty more under the surface for future generations that are better educated.'

45

Glossary

ancestor a person or animal that lived many years ago to which a human is related

ape a monkey-like animal that has a broader chest, no tail and a bigger brain than a monkey

archaeologist a scientist who studies the past by digging up artefacts

archaeological dig the process of digging in the ground to find objects and human remains, in order to study them

archaeological site a place where an archaeological dig takes place

archaeology the scientific study of objects and human remains found in the ground to learn about how man's ancestors lived their lives, and in the case of early humans, their physical appearance

artefact an object made or given shape by man, such as a tool or a work of art, that is of archaeological interest

descended came from

discarded thrown away

deoxyribonucleic acid (DNA) an extremely long, but very small, molecule that is the main component of chromosomes. This is the substance that contains all our genes, or characteristics

evolution the slow process whereby animals and other life forms change and adapt to suit their environment over hundreds of thousands or millions of years

excavate dig material out of the ground

expelled forced to leave

fossilisation the natural process whereby dead animals and other creatures are naturally preserved for hundreds of thousands or millions of years, usually buried underground

fragment a very small piece

hominid one of various species of early man that lived before *Homo sapiens*, for example, *Homo erectus* or *Homo habilis*

Homo sapiens the scientific name given to our species, the human race. Originally there were a number of different species of human, including *Homo erectus* and *Homo habilis*

pronounced extends outwards, highly visible or noticable

sapient appearing to be wise or human-like

sentient able to feel things

settlement an area or place where people choose to make their home

species a group of animals or plants that look like each other and can interbreed

temperament a type of personality

witnessed experienced or saw something first-hand

For More Information

Books

Early People (Eye Wonder), Jim Pipe, DK Children

Jane Goodall: Chimpanzee Protector (Women in Conservation), Robin S. Doak, Raintree

Jane Goodall: Researcher Who Champions Chimps (Getting to Know the World's Greatest Inventors and Scientists), Mike Venezia, Scholastic

Mary Leakey: Archaeologist Who Really Dug Her Work (Getting to Know the World's Greatest Inventors and Scientists), Mike Venezia, Scholastic

Websites and Films

The charity founded by Mary Leakey, which continues to give money to scientists who study our earliest ancestors, can be found at:
www.leakeyfoundation.org

Take a closer look at our early ancestors at the Natural History Museum's website:
www.nhm.ac.uk/nature-online/life/human-origins/early-human-family/index.html

Find out how you can join Jane Goodall's organisation and make a difference to the lives of animals and people around the world at:
www.rootsandshoots.org

Find out more about Jane Goodall and her story in the 2010 film *Jane's Journey*, by Lorenz Knauer.

Note to parents and teachers
Every effort has been made by the Publisher to ensure that these websites contain no inappropriate or offensive material. However, because of the nature of the Internet, it is impossible to guarantee that the contents of these sites will not be altered. We strongly advise that Internet access is supervised by a responsible adult.

Index